HONEYMOONERS

HONEYMOONERS

Starring the Kramdens and the Nortons

Bob Columbe

Illustrated by Howard Bender

An ILLUSTRATED TRIVIA Book

As You've Never Seen Them Before!

A PERIGEE BOOK

Also by Bob Columbe

The Official Honeymooners Treasury

Perigee Books
are published by
The Putnam Publishing Group
200 Madison Avenue
New York, NY 10016

*The publisher and the authors gratefully acknowledge
the assistance and cooperation of Viacom Enterprises.*

Designed by Susan Brooker/Levavi & Levavi

Library of Congress Cataloging-in-Publication Data

Columbe, Bob.
    Honeymooners: an illustrated trivia book.

    "A Perigee book."
    1. Honeymooners (Television program)—Miscellanea.
I. Title.
PN1992.77.H623C65   1986   791.45'72   86-21283
ISBN 0-399-51308-6 (pbk.)

PRINTED IN THE UNITED STATES OF AMERICA
1 2 3 4 5 6 7 8 9 10

ACKNOWLEDGMENTS

We'd like to thank the following people for their help, encouragement, and support for this project: Jackie Gleason, Richard Green, Esq., Kenneth D. Werner, Ginger McNamara, Joann DiGennaro, and our editor, Lee Ann Chearneyi, who is indeed a treasure.

HOW TO ENJOY THIS BOOK

Stop that bus; drop that bowling ball; pick up your Racoon cap and go!

Imagine yourself as a contestant on the *$99,000 Answer*—and your category is *The Honeymooners*. But make sure you've learned from Ralph's mistakes; stay calm, cool, and collected (unlike Ralph Kramden, the World's #1 Safe Dus Briver!). You'll find out just how much you *really* know about Ralph, Norton, Alice, and Trixie.

More thrilling than 3D television, cheaper than a share in Ralph's uranium mine in Asbury Park, more practical than the Handy Housewife Helper, *Honeymooners: An Illustrated Trivia Book* is the greatest new challenge for you *Honeymooners* fans everywhere. Va-va-va-voom!

For information on becoming a member of RALPH™ (The Royal Association for the Longevity and Preservation of the Honeymooners), the world-renowned *Honeymooners* fanclub, write to:

RALPH™
LIU / C. W. Post Campus
Greenvale, NY 11548

INTRODUCTION

What began as a casual lunchtime conversation almost four years ago (Bob: "Hey, Pete, did you ever watch *The Honeymooners*?" Pete: "*The Honeymooners*—Homina, homina, homina!") has become a national phenomenon—Honeymooner mania. When Peter Crescenti and I started RALPH (Royal Association for the Longevity and Preservation of the Honeymooners), our original goal was to get the "Classic 39" back on New York TV after a lengthy absence. Little did we know that the admiration and affection we felt for the Kramdens and the Nortons was shared by tens of thousands of people nationwide. The show came back to New York TV all right (eventually we even persuaded the station to run it seven nights a week in its original unedited form), and before you could say zip, zip, the modern way, Jackie Gleason had given us the original Ralph Kramden bus driver's uniform, RALPH's membership had grown to 10,000 plus, *The Honeymooners* was running in dozens of cities across the country, our campaign to get the lost episodes released was a success (thanks to Jackie Gleason and Viacom Enterprises), Honeymooners merchandise was on store shelves everywhere, and the entire country was "Kramden conscious."

Peter and I couldn't be happier. Unlike Kramden and Norton, we have hit the high note. The opportunity to meet Jackie Gleason, Art Carney, Audrey Meadows, Joyce Randolph, and dozens of other wonderful folks involved with *The Honeymooners* has been a thrill and a privilege. We have been amazed at the standing-room-only response to the Honeymooners con-

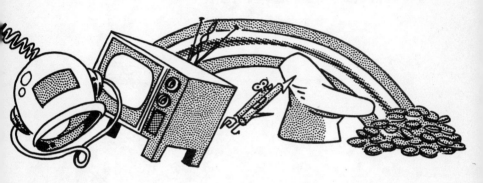

ventions we have hosted, and the success of our first book *The Official Honeymooners Treasury* has been tremendous. As we've always said, it just goes to prove that "every dog has his day."

And now, the book you are holding, *Honeymooners: An Illustrated Trivia Book*, is yet another proof of a "happier life through television," as Ed Norton once said. On the following pages you will find some of the greatest illustrations ever done from TV's most enduring show. Howard Bender, a RALPH member since the early days of the Club, is a true Honeymooners fan; such a fan, in fact, that when he was doing illustrations for *Superman* comics he used to sneak Honeymooners references into the panels! For this book, Howard has let his imagination run wild, illustrating sequences from both the "Classic 39" and the "Lost Episodes." You'll see the Kramdens and the Nortons as you've never seen them before, and you'll learn some amazing new facts: how the Kramdens and the Nortons first met; Trixie's real name; where Norton got his yellow shoes, and much more.

Howard and I had a lot of fun putting this book together; in fact, you could say it's been a regular riot. We hope you enjoy it.

Rx,
Bob Columbe
July 1986

THE KRAMDEN PHILOSOPHY

When they made me they threw away the mold.

Be kind to the people you meet on the way up, because you're going to meet the same people on the way down.

I am King in my Castle.

History repeats itself—Brutus had his Caesar, Kramden has his Norton.

When I'm in the right, I'm in the right—nobody pushes me around.

It's my nature to spend, the only trouble is, I never have anything to spend.

One hand washes the other hand and both hands wash the face.

Ralph Kramden will never be accused of not putting down a horse with a clock in its stomach.

If they get anything out of me, it won't be out of me that they get it.

I got a B-i-i-i-g Mouth!

SONGWRITERS

1 A professional songwriter writes a marching song for the Racoons. What is his affiliation with the lodge?

2 Fill in the blanks to the opening line of the Racoon's marching song: "From the _____ unto the _____ there's a mighty little _____."

3 Ralph thinks he can get rich writing songs when he hears how much the Racoons paid a songwriter to write their marching song. How much did the songwriter make?

4 Who does Ralph recruit as his songwriting partner and what instrument does he play?

5 Norton has to warm up before playing a song on the piano. How does he warm up?

6 True or false? Trixie calls Ralph and Norton the Bensonhurst Lerner and Loewe.

7 Ralph and Alice battle over the piano Ralph buys. Ralph compares his situation to that of a great composer who died and left behind an "unfinished symphony." Who was the composer?

8 Name the three kinds of songs Ralph and Norton try to write before scoring with a novelty song.

9 The boys take their song to a publisher who loves the _____ but hates the _____.

10 True or false? Ralph and Norton actually hit the high note: Their song is played on the radio.

THROUGH TV

A word-fill to test your skill.

B	E	L	L	E	V	U	E	O	P	A	Y	D	N	A	H
C	H	E	F	O	F	T	H	E	F	U	T	U	R	E	O
H	S	C	R	E	W	D	R	I	V	E	R	M	E	A	U
A	C	H	E	E	S	E	G	R	A	T	E	R	M	T	S
R	O	S	C	L	P	H	Z	O	N	O	T	R	O	N	E
L	R	C	O	R	E	A	A	P	P	L	E	S	V	B	W
I	K	U	R	H	A	H	A	E	T	O	L	C	E	S	I
E	S	T	K	O	R	S	D	N	Y	T	E	I	C	C	F
C	S	G	S	J	F	U	P	C	F	N	V	S	O	H	E
H	K	L	C	A	I	K	O	A	G	E	I	S	R	Z	H
A	A	A	R	M	S	L	S	N	L	D	S	O	N	L	E
N	T	S	E	A	H	H	N	S	N	M	I	R	S	J	L
D	E	S	W	Z	I	P	Z	I	P	A	O	S	X	Q	P
K	K	C	H	I	N	M	O	D	E	R	N	W	A	Y	E
L	E	M	Q	N	G	P	J	C	H	K	S	A	M	U	R
B	Y	A	T	G	S	S	C	A	L	E	F	I	S	H	O

AMAZING
BELLEVUE
CHARLIE CHAN
CHEESE GRATER
CHEF OF THE FUTURE
CORE A APPLE
CORKSCREW
CORKS
CUT GLASS
HA HA
HANDY HOUSEWIFE HELPER
KRAMDEN

MODERN WAY
NORTON
OPEN CANS
REMOVE CORNS
SCISSORS
SCALE FISH
SPEARFISHING
SCREWDRIVER
SKATE KEY
TELEVISION
ZIP ZIP

THE HANDY HOUSEWIFE HELPER

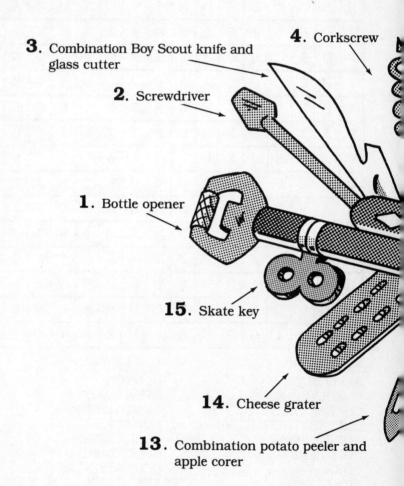

3. Combination Boy Scout knife and glass cutter

4. Corkscrew

2. Screwdriver

1. Bottle opener

15. Skate key

14. Cheese grater

13. Combination potato peeler and apple corer

5. Combination nail clipper and corn remover

6. Scissor sharpener

7. Razor

8. Can opener

9. Self-propelled spearfishing attachment

10. Pencil sharpener

11. Fish scaler

12. Tweezer

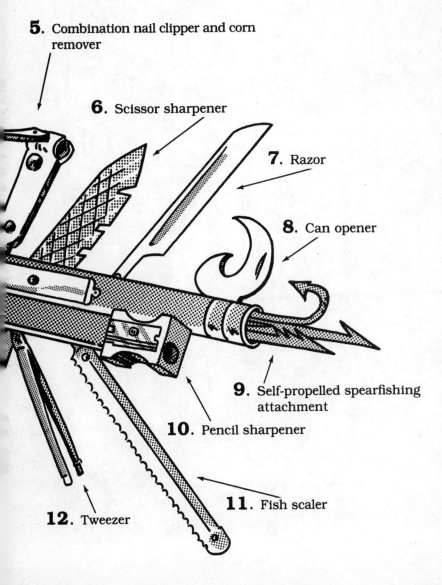

RALPH AND ALICE

Ralph could never remember just where he and Alice first met. At various times he told Norton he met her in school, in a cafeteria, and when they both worked for the W.P.A.—Ralph shoveling snow and Alice handing out the shovels.

Ralph and Alice were the Fred Astaire and Ginger Rogers of Brooklyn. On their first date, they went dancing at the Hotel New Yorker. When the Sons of Italy Hall had dance bands (Isham Jones, Ted Fio Rito, Little Jack Little, Basil Fomeen, Johnny Messler and His Toy Piano) they used to go dancing there. They danced at the Colonnade Room ("I can do the fox-trot, but when it comes to the mambo or samba, I'm out") and the Racoon Lodge costume party ("Nobody does the peabody like me"). They both did the hula—Alice in an amateur show and Ralph at a party with a lampshade on his head. Ralph took hucklebuck lessons from Norton and both Ralph and Alice took mambo lessons from Carlos Sanchez. Whew!

After an evening of dancing they would go to a Chinese restaurant, order Alice's favorite appetizer (sweet and sour li-chee nuts), have chop suey and fried rice, and con the waiter into bringing them bread ("This is a Chinese restaurant, we have no bread here").

Official Space Helmet

on Captain Video!

THE GOLFER

How well can you address this match-up quiz?

1. What do you say to a fox?

2. Mr. Harper

3. Where does Ralph play golf?

4. It don't mean a thing if ___.

5. How do you address a golf ball?

6. Emily

7. Mr. Douglas

8. Tell him you're smart but ___.

9. Where does Mr. Harper play golf?

10. a pincushion

11. pots and pans

A. hello ball

B. has an inspiring slice

C. up hill and down hill

D. you ain't got no good connections

E. tallyho

F. V.P. of the Gotham Bus Company

G. Traffic Manager at the Gotham Bus Company

H. you ain't got that swing

I. all around

J. Silver Oaks

K. chicken noodles

EDWARD L. NORTON

Edward L. Norton (the L. stands for Lilywhite) is a man of many talents and accomplishments:

MUSICIAN—He plays the piano, harmonica, and cornet.

DANCER—He won a pair of yellow shoes in a mambo contest.

COMPOSER—He wrote the melody for "My Love Song to You."

THESPIAN—He played Hamilton Douglas in the Racoon Lodge play.

ATHLETE—He bowls, shoots pool, plays punchball, and coaches stickball.

MATHEMATICIAN—He majored in math at vocational school.

VETERAN—He served in the navy and studied typing under the G.I. Bill.

ANTIQUE COLLECTOR—He owns a genuine four-legged Chippendale.

EXECUTIVE—He is Vice-President and Chairman of the Board of Ralph Kramden, Inc.

CLUB MAN—He is Sergeant at Arms in the Racoon Lodge, a ranger third class in the Captain Video Space Academy, and a member of the Mickey Mouse Club.

And, in his current capacity (about 50,000 gallons), he is an engineer in subterranean sanitation.

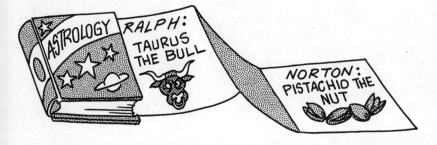

While Mr. Norton has been known to quote Shakespeare and Dickens, his personal philosophy is revealed through a study of his own pronouncements:

Time and tide wait for no man.

As you slide down the bannister of life, may the splinters never be facing the wrong way.

A sewer worker is like a brain surgeon, we're both specialists.

Compared to a clam, I am an oyster.

If manhole covers were pizzas, the sewer would be a paradise.

> A man don't look at himself like others see him.

If I had any sense of smell do you think I would work in a sewer?

> A slip of a lip can sink a ship and I never sunk one.

> We stick together in the sewer. We have a motto: Water is thicker than blood.

A MATTER OF LIFE AND DEATH

1 Where does Norton want Ralph to go with him to get a few "practice shots"?

2 Ralph, feeling tired, has gone to the doctor for a checkup. He tells Norton he hopes there is a little something wrong with him so he can "lay off" for how long?

3 The doctor sends Ralph some pills. How are they supposed to be taken?

4 Ralph, thinking he has only six months to live, sits down to make out his will. Norton says making out a will is pretty important, otherwise all of Ralph's possessions might go where?

5 The publishers of *American Weekly* magazine are excited about doing Ralph's story. They think they can make him a national hero, another ____ ____.

6 When Ralph realizes he isn't going to die, he's afraid the *American Weekly* people will send him to prison. For how long?

7 Ralph tells Norton he isn't going to die. What is Norton's startled response?

8 When Ralph faints and Norton thinks he is dead, what three articles of clothing does Norton lament that Ralph won't be wearing anymore?

9 After Ralph cons Norton into posing as a doctor who can cure arterial monochromia, Norton cautions Ralph: "Don't touch me, I'm ____!"

10 Mr. Gersh, the publisher of *American Weekly*, says Ralph's story is really selling papers. The whole country is "____ ____."

WET CARDS ARE WILD

1 Knuckle-knuckle, a favorite card game of the boys in the sewer, has an unusual rule: Wet cards are wild!

2 Norton's boss once caught a giant marlin in the sewer—and killed it in self-defense!

3 When a guy and a girl are going steady, the guy usually gives his pin to his girl. They have a similar custom in the sewer—carving your best girl's initials on the handle of your shovel.

4 Norton has trouble lighting his cigar when he's on the job because "in the sewer, there ain't no dry end."

5 Even though they work in the sewer, the boys still manage to play dice on their lunch hour—sort of a floating crap game.

6 Norton always catches a cold when he works in the Park Avenue sewer—it's air-conditioned!

7 Norton always beats Ralph at Ping-Pong. He acquired his skill playing in the sewer—it's the only game they can play with a ball that floats.

8 Every job has its occupational hazards; when you're a sewer worker, it's a manhole cover landing on your head.

KRAMDEN VS. NORTON

FREE TV DRAWING

 It's Norton's birthday, Ralph and Alice are taking him out, and Ralph's in a dither. Why?

2 When it was Ralph's birthday Norton took him to the Kit Kat Club. Where does Ralph want to take Norton for his birthday?
- A. bowling
- B. the National Racoon Mambo Championship
- C. the movies
- D. Salvatore's pizzeria

3 Name the people who give Norton birthday gifts and identify the gifts.

4 The "L." in Edward L. Norton stands for:
A. Larry
B. Lenny
C. Lilywhite
D. Lester

5 "Diamond Jim" Kramden takes Alice and the Nortons to the movies to celebrate Norton's birthday. What movie do they see?

6 True or false? Norton wins a set of dishes in a raffle at the movies.

7 Ralph and Norton feud over ownership of the prize Norton won at the movies. Things get so bad the two communicate by writing notes to each other and they even ____ ____ with their wives instead of with each other.

8 Ralph and Norton go to night court to settle their dispute. The judge is well known for two roles he played in the "Classic 39." What were they?

9 To Norton's surprise, Trixie reveals on the witness stand that her real name is ____.

10 According to the story Alice tells the judge, how did the Kramdens and the Nortons meet?

ALICE

When Ralph accuses Alice of not keeping up on the latest developments, she counters with ". . . not up on the latest developments, who is it that lets your pants out every other day?"

Ralph was a dreamer—big dreams, dreams as big as his waistline, the-pot-of-gold-at-the-end-of-the-rainbow type dreams. But as far as Alice was concerned, Ralph's big dreams were nothing more than crazy schemes—crazy harebrained schemes—doomed to failure. Schemes like wallpaper that glows in the dark, the uranium mine in Asbury Park, and no-cal pizza had all been flops. But Ralph was certain he had a winner with the Handy Housewife Helper, a kitchen gadget with numerous features. Needing money to finance a TV commercial to sell them, he pleads with Alice to give him the money, telling her "this is probably the biggest thing I ever got into." Alice, in a calm and perfectly logical manner, responds with a classic retort, "The biggest thing you ever got into was your pants."

When Ralph and Alice got married, Alice's mother took great delight in telling everyone at the wedding, "I'm not losing a daughter, I'm gaining a ton."

In a typical Kramden argument about money—Ralph wants it and Alice won't give it to him—Ralph accuses Alice of spending all his hard-earned money on clothes. To prove his point he opens Alice's bureau drawer, which is full of her clothes. He then opens his drawer and finds just one pair of pants in it. Sensing victory, he demands to know why her drawer is full of clothes and his drawer has only one pair of pants. Alice, as usual, cuts Ralph down to size when she replies, "One pair of your pants is all that will fit in that drawer."

BROTHER RALPH

1 Ralph is laid off at the bus company because of a suggestion he made. What was it?

2 When it looks like there's going to be a money crunch in the Kramden household, Alice tells Ralph he'd better stop spending money on something. What?

3 How much money do the Kramdens have saved and how much do they owe in bills?

4 Alice decides she has to get a job. What skills does she have?

5 Her first week on the job Alice has to work overtime. What does she have to do?

6 Name Alice's boss and her co-workers.

7 True or false? When Ralph hears that Alice works only with men at the office, he figures she must be a riot around the coffee pot.

8 True or false? When Ralph, who is posing as Alice's brother, finds out that Alice's boss wants a date with her, he tells him Alice is already dating an engineer in subterranean sanitation.

9 Alice's boss wants to drive Alice home in his convertible, but Ralph offers to tag along and bring Alice home on the _____ instead.

10 Who brings Ralph the news that his layoff is over?
   A. Freddie
   B. Charlie
   C. Grogan
   D. Garrity

THE ADOPTION

1 The Kramdens want to adopt a child. What does the adoption agency want to see before okaying the Kramdens' application?
   A. the apartment
   B. Ralph's pay stub
   C. Ralph's tax return
   D. Ralph's social security number

2 True or false? In order to impress the adoption agency people, the Kramdens move into the Norton's apartment.

3 Who comes from the agency to visit the Kramdens?
   A. Miss Lawrence
   B. Tony Amico
   C. Mrs. Stevens
   D. Millie Davis

4 What does Ralph see inside the refrigerator he borrows that surprises him?

5 The Kramdens are approved by the adoption agency and will get a baby. But when they go to the hospital to pick up the baby, Ralph wants to give it back because it's a _____.

6 What do the Kramdens name the baby?

7 Ralph can't stop buying the baby:
   A. pizza
   B. raccoon caps
   C. dolls
   D. bowling balls

8 Ralph buys the baby a doll that dances the hucklebuck. True or false?

9 When Ralph can't find a nipple to put on a bottle to feed the baby, what does Norton suggest he use instead?

10 Why do the Kramdens give up the baby?

THE SAFETY AWARD

1 What is the name of the magazine that is doing a story on Ralph being named the city's safest bus driver?

2 Whose idea was it to put a plaque on Ralph's bus stating "You Are Now Riding with the City's Safest Bus Driver"?

3 Ralph is to receive his award at City Hall. Whose car does he borrow to drive there?

4 Alice and Trixie are wearing identical polka-dot dresses. What store did they buy them at?

5 When Ralph and Norton realize they are wearing identical sport jackets, an argument develops. Who finally gives in and changes his jacket?

6 Norton wants to borrow one of Ralph's new handkerchiefs. Ralph gives it to him, reluctantly, but cautions him "_____."

7 What happens to Trixie on the way to the car?

8 What happens to Ralph on the way to City Hall?

9 Because the Commissioner has the flu, Judge Lawrence Norton Hurdle (probably, as an inside joke, named after *Honeymooners* producer Jack Hurdle) is to present Ralph with his award. What is "Hollerin' Hurdle" noted for?

10 After Ralph receives his award, why does he want to take Alice, Trixie, and Norton upstairs at City Hall?

THE RACOON LODGE

Woo-Woooooo! That's the greeting of the Racoon Lodge, a national organization with a chapter in Bensonhurst and a cemetery in Bismarck, North Dakota. An entire book could be written about this fine and noble organization, but for now here are some vital facts about the Racoons:

The Racoon Lodge was originally known as the International Order of Friendly Sons of the Racoons. It later became known, among other titles, as the International Order of Loyal Racoons, and the International Order of Friendly Racoons. To Alice Kramden, it's just "that silly lodge."

The Grand High Exalted Mystic Ruler of the Racoons is Morris Fink.

Ralph Kramden is Treasurer (he got elected by pledging to use the lodge's surplus funds to buy beer and hot dogs) and once served as the head of the ticket committee for the Racoons' dance.

Norton has served as both Secretary and Sergeant at Arms.

The Racoons' slogan is "E Pluribus Racoon."

The two men credited with founding the Racoons are Toots Mondello and Herman Hildebrand.

The Racoons have held national conventions in Chicago and in Minneapolis.

The Racoons' toast is "Fingers to fingers, thumbs to thumbs, watch out below, here she comes!"

Jackie Gleason once appeared at the Racoons' annual dance. (Alice got him there after Ralph bragged to the Racoons that he knew Gleason. He didn't.)

The lodge's monthly dues are $2; the initiation fee is $1.50.

THE LOUDSPEAKER/ GUEST SPEAKER

"The Loudspeaker," the episode from the "Classic 39" in which Ralph thinks he's being named Racoon of the Year, is based on the 1953 short skit, "Guest Speaker." In both episodes Ralph gets a message that he should be prepared to speak at that night's Racoon meeting. And in typical Kramden fashion, he jumps to the conclusion least likely to be true.

"THE LOUDSPEAKER"
APRIL 21,1956

Here's a comparison of the two episodes:

"The Loudspeaker"—April 21, 1956

Ralph thinks he's being named Racoon of the Year and he prepares his acceptance speech. He is hummmmble!

> It's actually Norton who's named Racoon of the Year.

> Morris Fink, the Grand High Exalted Mystic Ruler, works in the sewer with Norton.

Ralph plans to break up the meeting with a joke he made up about King Arthur and Sir Lancelot.

> The Racoon of the Year is eligible to run for Grand High Exalted Mystic Ruler.

> Racoon of the Year wears platinum braid on his uniform, opens the first clam at the annual Racoon clambake, steers as the Racoons sail past Racoon Point, and is entitled to free burial at the National Racoon Cemetery in Bismarck, North Dakota. He also has the option of throwing the first bag of water out the hotel window at the Racoon convention.

"GUEST SPEAKER"
JUNE 13, 1953

This skit ran only 13 minutes and 31 seconds.

The lodge is known as the International Order of Friendly Sons of the Racoons.

Norton isn't a member of the lodge.

Ralph doesn't think he's being named Racoon of the Year, but he does think he's been picked to make an important speech.

George Williams is head of the Bensonhurst Racoons. Ralph discovers at the end of the episode that all he has to do is introduce George.

Ralph's joke is going to be about the Racoons working like beavers.

At the end of both episodes, Alice assures a disappointed Ralph that he's still the #1 Racoon in their house.

WEIGHTY PROBLEM

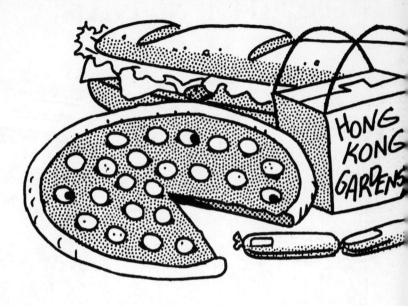

All the world may love a fat man, but for Ralph Kramden being fat is no joke. For instance, in one episode Norton claims Ralph wears a girdle; and Ralph can only bristle when Alice says Ralph wanted to but couldn't find one that fit. In the lost episode, "Weighty Problem," Ralph spends all his time in a battle of the bulge:

1 Who tells Ralph he's too fat to drive a bus?

2 At the bus company a six-foot-tall driver may weight up to _____ pounds. A five-foot-eleven driver must weigh no more than _____ pounds.

3 Ralph goes on a diet. He tells Alice he lost a pound and she says that Ralph losing a pound is like Bayonne losing a _____.

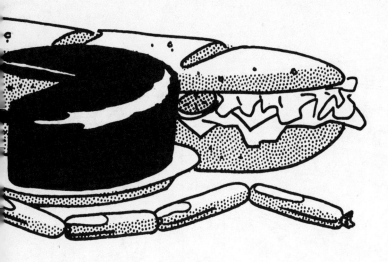

4 Ralph hangs on to his diet for dear life until he finds some food left in the apartment by a neighbor. Who is the neighbor and what food did she leave at the Kramdens'?

In "Ralph's Diet," a shorter, earlier lost episode upon which "Weighty Problem" was based, we learn why Ralph hates dieting: It's the food he has to eat! Here's a sample of Ralph's diet menu:

　　Breakfast—one poached egg, half a grapefruit
　　Lunch—one hard-boiled egg, two stalks of celery, an apple
　　Dinner—raw vegetable salad

And what is Ralph's reaction to this diet fare? He tells Alice, "I've seen more food than that dragged down holes by ants!!!"

BROTHER-IN-LAW

1 Which of Alice's brothers does Ralph hate?

2 Why does Ralph consider Alice's brother "a moocher, a chiseler, and a bum"?

3 Alice's brother tries to put the bite on the Kramdens for money? How much?

4 True or false? Alice wants to give her brother the money.

5 Alice's brother has a scheme that can't be put into operation without the money from the Kramdens. Ralph won't lend him the money but he loves the scheme. What is it?

6 The hotel Ralph wants to buy is located in Weehawken, New Jersey. True or false?

7 The hotel looks like Yucca Flats after the blast. But how does Norton describe it?

8 Match the person with the job:
Ralph   chef
Alice   manager
Norton   chambermaid
Trixie   bellhop

9 Who is the first guest to register in the hotel?

10 True or false? A new highway is being built that will go right past the hotel and make the Kramdens and the Nortons lots of money.

TRIXIE

Trixie's real name is Thelma—something even Norton didn't know until she revealed it under oath on the witness stand when Ralph and Norton sued each other to determine the ownership of a TV set.

Norton and Trixie met when she was dancing in a burlesque show. Norton brought her a rose, which she used as a costume. Norton is proud of her burlesque background, boasting to Ralph that "Trixie was the original end girl in the Floogle Street sketch."

When the Nortons were married, they hitchhiked to Niagara Falls for their honeymoon.

"You can take the man out of the sewer, but you can't take the sewer out of the man."

Trixie Norton—1955

OH MY ACHING BACK

1   Alice wants Ralph to go with her to her mother's house. Ralph lies to her about staying home but he really plans to go bowling. What's the occasion?

2   Why is Ralph's bowling team so anxious to beat the rival team?

3   After Ralph has a fight with Alice about going bowling he tells Norton he's staying home and Norton should find another bowler to take his place. Who?

4   The Racoons have a victory dinner ready for them if they win the match. Who prepared it and what did he make?

5 Which Racoon invited his mother over from Canarsie to watch the match?

6 Which Racoon is soon to be married (provided the team doesn't take a shellacking)?

7 Ralph bowls, the team wins, and Ralph hurts his:
A. head
B. neck
C. back
D. sacroiliac

 Ralph feels terrible so Norton takes his temperature. When he can't see the red line on the thermometer, he uses a match to help him see it. True or false?

 Who visits Ralph and almost puts him in the hospital by repeatedly slapping him on the back?

 Who brings Ralph his trophy as the team's most valuable player?

KRAMDEN'S GREAT SCHEMES

In "Finders Keepers," Ralph and Norton meet at the neighborhood candy store, and within seconds another spat breaks out between them—this one over a pinball game and a box of candy. But they soon find something to soothe their bruised feelings and restore peace to Bensonhurst—another crazy scheme. This time Ralph and Norton want to buy a candy store!

In the lost episodes, just as in the "Classic 39," Ralph is forever chasing the Big Score, and most of the time he drags Norton along for the ride. Here are some of Ralph's best schemes from the lost episodes:

Managing a heavyweight boxer who turns out to have a glass jaw.

Entering a talent contest with Norton to win $200.

Investing $300 (Norton drops $200 on this one) in a phony hair restorer.

Buying a dilapidated hotel in New Jersey.

Buying a hot dog stand in New Jersey.

Entering box-top contests.

Investing in pills that are supposed to turn water into gasoline.

Starting a no-cal pizza business.

And then there were two schemes Ralph wanted to invest in with his brother, but he couldn't raise the money: a used-tire store and a rug-shampooing business!

$99,000 ANSWER

As a boy, Ralph sold lemonade, delivered groceries for the A & P, took cornet lessons, and even studied architecture. But when the Charleston came along he forgot about everything else and began to frequent ballrooms and listen to dance bands, becoming an expert on popular songs. "I know all there is to know about popular songs," he tells Alice.

Let's see if you know all there is to know about the "$99,000 Answer":

 Mr. Parker, the contestant who precedes Ralph, chose what category?

 When the quiz master, Herb Norris, asks Ralph what his wife's name is, Ralph replies "_____."

 Herb Norris hopes Ralph wins some money because he has something for Ralph. What is it?

 Trixie tells Alice that Ralph should face the camera because when he stands profile, "_____, _____."

5 Alice pleads with Ralph not to stay home from work and rent a piano "that will take every cent we have in the bank." Ralph responds, "When the smoke clears away _____."

6 Who wants to see the look on Ralph's face when he misses the $99,000 question?

7 Before Norton begins to play the piano he takes out his handkerchief. What does he do with it?

8 Alice wants Norton to stop playing the piano, but Ralph wants him to continue. Norton, in a predicament, raises his arms and asks, "_____?"

9 When Ralph returns for his second appearance on the show, he is relaxed and full of confidence. In reply to Herb Norris's inquiry as to whether he spent his spare time "brushing up" on popular songs, Ralph boasts "_____."

10 Ralph misses the first question ("Who was the composer of 'Swanee River'?"), and his dream of winning $99,000 goes up in smoke. He leaves the show without "peanuts" or a "mere bag of shells." How much was the first question worth?

THE WORRY WART

If they get anything out of Ralph, it won't be out of Ralph that they get it! Can you get the match-ups below?

1. the Kramdens' icebox
2. Mrs. Schwartz
3. amount Ralph won shooting pool
4. amount Ralph won playing poker
5. Mr. Puder
6. the Collier Brothers
7. Freddy Muller
8. Dizzy Dean
9. Kramden's gas bill
10. Kramden's bank balance
11. Fred's tent
12. Ralph's Christmas bonus

A. has a snake in it
B. a skinny chicken
C. $85
D. 39¢
E. a blabbermouth
F. early Ma & Pa Kettle
G. low gas bill in 1931
H. IRS officer
I. $75
J. $25
K. warms up in the bull pen
L. executive at the Gotham Bus Company

SONGS AND WITTY SAYINGS

1 Ralph and Norton plan to enter a talent contest at the Racoon Lodge. True or false?

2 What's first prize for winning the contest?
  A. $99,000
  B. Peanuts; peanuts!
  C. $200
  D. $12.83

3 Name the three things that make up Ralph and Norton's act.

4 Alice and Trixie are entering the contest too. What's their act?

5 Trixie used to be in burlesque and she originated a role in a famous comedy routine. What is the routine?

6 Ralph is dead-set against Alice entering the amateur contest. But Alice appeals to Ralph's pride and he not only changes his mind about her entering the contest, but bets her he and Norton will win it. What are the terms of the bet?

7 True or false? Ralph and Norton rehearse Abbott and Costello impersonations for the talent contest.

8 The first contestant is:
  A. Thelma, the maid
  B. Frank, Bill, Pete, and George
  C. the Grand High Exalted Mystic Ruler
  D. the delivery boy from Freitag's

9 Ralph and Norton do a mind-reading act. What object does Norton try to guess?

10 Alice and Trixie win the contest and they buy dinner to celebrate. Dinner is:
  A. pizza from Salvatore's
  B. Chinese food
  C. pig's knuckles and sauerkraut
  D. chicken chow mein and potato pancakes

MY FAIR LANDLORD

Norton's been called a nut, a mental case, a moax, a dope, and a stupid head. But deep down he's nothing but an overgrown kid. Why else would he plan his life around episodes of *Captain Video*? In the lost episode "My Fair Landlord," we discover Norton's not only a space cadet, but a merry Mouseketeer too!

1 Ralph gets fed up with things at Chauncey Street, so he decides to buy a house. To what New York borough does he move?
   A. Bronx
   B. Manhattan
   C. Staten Island
   D. Queens

2 True or false? The Kramdens recruit the Nortons as tenants in the new house.

3 How long is the lease Norton signs with Ralph?

4 Norton discovers something about the basement in the new house that probably warms his heart. What is it?

5 In his lease with Norton, Ralph is known as the:
   A. mope
   B. Racoon of the Year
   C. party of the first part
   D. dirty bum

6 Norton wants the molding in his apartment painted gray. What shade of gray?

7 While Ralph is painting the apartment Norton watches TV. He watches:
   A. Captain Video
   B. Charlie Chan
   C. Liberace
   D. Mickey Mouse Club

8 True or false? When Norton tells Ralph to hurry up with the painting, Ralph gets Alice to help him finish the job.

9 Norton wants Ralph to rip up his lease because he's fed up with Ralph. What is his plan to get kicked out of the apartment?

10 Ralph almost gets thrown in jail for banging a huge ____ with a ____ in the middle of the night.

RALPH KRAMDEN, INC.

1 Norton, the bird watcher, claims he watches birds because they watch him. Ralph says the only bird that watches Norton is a _____.

2 How much money does Ralph want Norton to invest in the Ralph Kramden Corporation?

3 Norton joins Ralph Kramden, Inc., as Vice-President with a 20 percent interest. How long is it until Norton cons Ralph into giving him a larger percentage?

4 When Ralph learns that he is mentioned in the will of Mary Monahan, the old lady he used to help on the bus, and that her estate is worth $40 million, what is his reaction? What is Norton's reaction?

5 How many living relatives does Mary Monahan mention in her will?

6 Ralph tells Alice that Norton is the nervous type; if he came into money he would go _____.

7 According to Norton, what percentage of the $40 million belongs to the stockholders?

8 Mary Monahan's parrot, Fortune, is so upset at her death it won't eat its _____.

9 In her will, Mary Monahan describes Ralph as having four attributes. What are they?

10 What is Ralph's reaction to inheriting Fortune, the parrot? What is Norton's?

THE SLEEPWALKER

A word-fill to test your skill.

T	S	R	A	P	P	L	E	P	M	N	C	E	L	Y	B
K	B	M	O	P	B	A	L	E	O	B	F	S	K	Z	A
M	E	N	T	A	L	C	P	N	B	D	H	Q	J	O	N
K	L	N	R	Q	O	R	E	T	T	E	S	U	B	B	A
O	L	T	U	V	C	C	S	A	A	G	N	I	A	A	N
S	S	A	Z	O	K	O	A	T	C	I	U	R	C	D	A
C	H	I	C	K	E	N	C	H	O	W	M	E	I	N	P
I	W	T	U	N	N	E	L	O	F	L	O	V	E	N	E
U	P	E	E	L	S	Y	U	L	F	U	J	D	B	J	E
S	W	N	T	A	W	I	N	J	H	L	W	A	R	M	L
Z	A	T	A	C	K	S	T	O	S	U	I	E	J	I	H
K	L	H	M	C	C	L	O	S	K	E	Y	S	N	L	S
O	K	A	V	S	B	A	N	A	N	A	K	F	P	K	S
S	I	R	Q	R	D	N	R	O	C	P	O	P	Q	B	T
O	N	Z	S	B	J	D	I	C	K	T	R	A	C	E	Y
G	G	K	U	M	Q	U	A	T	S	L	X	Z	T	A	C

APPLE	McCLOSKEYS
BELL	MENTAL BLOCK
BANANA PEEL	PENTATHOL
CHICKEN CHOW MEIN	POPCORN
CONEY ISLAND	TACKS
DICK TRACEY	TUNNEL OF LOVE
ESQUIRE	SETTER
KOSCIUSZKO	SLEEPWALKING
KUMQUATS	WARM MILK
LULU	

YOUNG AT HEART

1 Judy Connors, a teenage girl who lives in the Kramdens' apartment building, is waiting for her boyfriend, Wallace, to pick her up in his "frantic hot rod that's ready to percolate." What is Wallace's nickname? What is Judy's nickname?

2 Judy and Wallace are going to the amusement park, roller skating, the tunnel of love, and a _____ dance contest.

3 Alice called Ralph "icky." Ralph, perplexed, asked Norton what "icky" means. Norton replies, "It must mean _____."

4 Ralph is going to learn all the latest expressions to prove to Alice that he is hep. For example: "23 skidoo," "voh-de-oh-doh," and "I'll kiss you later, _____."

5 Norton, a man of many talents, is also a dancing master. What dance does he try to teach Ralph?

6 Norton tells Ralph to listen to the record and do what the lyric says—wiggle like a snake and waddle like a duck. Ralph complains that he can't waddle like a duck, to which Norton replies, "_____."

7 Ralph and Norton, in an attempt to recapture their youth, take Alice and Trixie roller skating. What is the name of the skating rink?

8 When Ralph and Alice were dating they used to go to dances that featured the bands of Basil Fomeen and Little Jack Little. Where were the dances held?

A DOG'S LIFE

1 The Kramdens' upstairs neighbor, _____ _____, is going to take Alice's dog to get its shots.

2 Even though Norton had a dog, Lulu, when he was a boy, he doesn't have one now because according to Trixie he is allergic to _____.

3 In addition to his boss, Mr. Marshall, Ralph also gives Kranmar's Delicious Mystery Appetizer to Mr. _____ and Mr. _____, two executives at the bus company.

4 To verify that Kranmar's Delicious Mystery Appetizer is actually dog food, the Gotham Bus Company's resident dog expert, _____, is called in to test it.

5 When Ralph realizes his blunder, he _____.

6 Trixie suggests to Alice that she give her dog one of those cute _____ names.

7 When Ralph asks Norton how he would feel if he gave dog food to his boss to eat, Norton replies, "Terrible, unless my boss was a _____ _____."

8 As Ralph leaves the apartment to return the puppy to the pound, Norton tells him, "Ralph Kramden, you have just lost your membership card to the _____ _____."

9 Alice, arriving at the pound and anxious to get her puppy back, is told she must speak to Mr. _____.

10 When Ralph leaves the pound, he not only has Alice's puppy, but _____ additional dogs as well.

BATTLE OF THE SEXES

1 True or false? Ralph and Norton are playing pool and Norton is snacking on pretzels. Ralph doesn't want any because he wants to stop for Neapolitan knockwurst on the way home.

2 Trixie calls Norton at the poolroom because she wants him to come home. Why?

3 How many nights a week do Ralph and Norton go out together and what do they do?

4 Ralph gives Norton his famous "King of the Castle" speech to encourage Norton to stand up to Trixie. What is the key phrase Ralph gives Norton to put Trixie in her place?
    A. "A slip of a lip will sink a ship."
    B. "You are a blabbermouth!"
    C. "I'm king of the castle and you're nothin'!"
    D. "I'll kiss you later, I'm eatin' a potato."

Norton gives Trixie the "king" speech and she crowns him. True or false?

 Norton and Ralph become roomies when their wives leave them. Ralph becomes the cook and he prepares a dish even iron-stomach Norton complains about. What is it?

 To help pass the time while they're doing household chores, Norton and Ralph dance around the apartment and sing. What song do they sing and dance to?
A. "Ragg Mopp"
B. "The Hucklebuck"
C. "I Had a Dream, Dear"
D. "Too Marvelous for Words"

While Ralph and Norton subsist on food from cans, Alice and Trixie feast upstairs. Trixie has prepared:
A. chicken à la Fensterblau
B. turkey
C. duck
D. goose

 Ralph is too proud to apologize to Alice so he schemes to get her back home. Name three routines he tries to trick Alice into moving back downstairs.

 Everyone knows you can't compare pot roast to Alice's kisses. So, when the Kramdens make up, Ralph rushes straight into Alice's arms for a kiss. True or false?

ANSWERS

SONGWRITERS

1. His father-in-law is a Racoon in Bayonne.
2. West; East; beast
3. $100
4. Norton; piano
5. He plays the introduction to "Swanee River."
6. False—it's Gilbert and Sullivan.
7. Schubert
8. love song; lullaby; holiday song
9. music; words
10. True

THE GOLFER

1. E
2. G
3. I
4. H
5. A
6. B
7. F
8. D
9. J
10. K
11. C

A MATTER OF LIFE AND DEATH

1. the bowling alley
2. a couple of weeks
3. in a saucer of warm milk
4. into escrow
5. Davy Crockett
6. twenty years
7. "You mean never?"
8. socks, hat, and pants
9. sterile
10. Kramden conscious

KRAMDEN VS. NORTON

1. Alice didn't get his shoes repaired, his long underwear froze on the clothesline, and he can't find his sweater.
2. C
3. Trixie—a new vest; the boys in the sewer—a mahogany surf board; Ralph and Alice—a monogrammed scarf.
4. C
5. *The Desert Hawk*
6. False—a television set.
7. play pool
8. Uncle Leo and Hollerin' Hurdle
9. Thelma
10. The day the Kramdens moved into the apartment building, Norton invited them out to dinner.

BROTHER RALPH

1. Hire a traffic expert
2. Bowling
3. They have $12.83; they owe $186.32.
4. She can type and take shorthand.
5. She has to do inventory sheets.
6. Tony Amico is the boss. Frank, Bill, Pete, and George are the co-workers.
7. False—the watercooler.
8. False—a prizefighter.
9. subway
10. A

THE ADOPTION

1. A
2. False—they borrow the Nortons' furniture.
3. A
4. He is surprised by the refrigerator light.
5. girl
6. Ralphina
7. C
8. False—the mambo.
9. a rubber glove
10. The natural mother wants the baby back and the Kramdens give her up even though Ralphina is legally theirs.

THE SAFETY AWARD

1. *Universal Magazine*
2. Ralph's
3. Freddy Muller's
4. Bloomgarten's
5. Ralph
6. "That's for showin', not blowin'."
7. The heel of her shoe breaks.
8. He has an auto accident.
9. Fifty-dollar fines and fifty-minute lectures.
10. to meet the Mayor

WEIGHTY PROBLEM

1. A Gotham Bus Company inspector.
2. 250; 238
3. mosquito
4. Mrs. Manicotti; a ham, a turkey, and a birthday cake for Mr. Manicotti's surprise birthday party.

BROTHER-IN-LAW

1. Frank
2. He cheated Ralph out of a promotion at the W.P.A.
3. $500
4. False—for once she sides with Ralph.
5. Buy a beaten-up hotel in New Jersey.
6. False—Crestwood.
7. Norton says it looks like the set of a Bela Lugosi movie.
8. Ralph   manager
   Alice   chef
   Norton   bellhop
   Trixie   chambermaid
9. George Petrie
10. False—the highway is being built above the hotel and cars will pass right over it.

OH MY ACHING BACK

1. His team, the Hurricanes, are bowling against the Racoons from Bayonne.
2. The Bayonne Racoons beat them in the National Racoon Mambo Championship.
3. Schultz
4. Herman Gruber is the chef. Three kinds of pizza, pig's knuckles and sauerkraut, and Neapolitan knockwurst is the menu.
5. Freddie
6. Eddie Mulloy
7. C
8. False—a cigarette lighter.
9. Uncle Leo
10. Freddie and Charlie

$99,000 ANSWER

1. currencies of the world
2. Mrs. Kramden
3. a cleaning bill for the suit Ralph splashed mud on
4. "Brother, he's the biggest thing on television."
5. ". . . there'll be $99,000."
6. Mrs. Gibson, Ralph's mother-in-law.
7. He brushes the dust from the chair and the piano keys.
8. "Why oh why was I blessed with this musical talent?"
9. "No sense going over what you already know."
10. $100

THE WORRY WART

1. F
2. E
3. J
4. C
5. H
6. G
7. L
8. K
9. D
10. I
11. A
12. B

SONGS AND WITTY SAYINGS

1. False—the Halsey Theater.
2. C
3. mind-reading act, jokes, song and dance
4. Trixie, dressed as a sailor, plays a ukulele while Alice, dressed as a hula girl, dances.
5. The Floogle Street sketch
6. They bet $10 and Ralph says he'll eat Alice's grass skirt if he loses.
7. False—Laurel and Hardy.
8. D
9. a ring
10. B

MY FAIR LANDLORD

1. D
2. True
3. 99 years
4. It's full of water.
5. C

6. He wants the gray to be the same shade as the retina of Ricardo Cortez's eyes.
7. D
8. False—he throws the cans of paint against the walls.
9. Norton and Trixie get up in the middle of the night and toot horns, shout, and use noisemakers to wake up Ralph.
10. tub, hammer

RALPH KRAMDEN, INC.

1. woodpecker
2. $20
3. a week
4. Ralph faints. Norton faints too!
5. one
6. nuts
7. 35 percent
8. breakfast
9. He is kind, courteous, sober, and conscientious.
10. Ralph faints. Norton faints too!

YOUNG AT HEART

1. Wallace is "Super Atomic Passion." Judy is "Angel Cake."
2. bop
3. fat
4. I'm eating a potato
5. The hucklebuck
6. "Just walk the way you always do."
7. Good Skates
8. The Sons of Italy Hall

A DOG'S LIFE

1. Mrs. Manicotti
2. fur
3. Peck; Tebbets
4. Charlie
5. faints
6. French
7. cocker spaniel
8. human race
9. MacGregor
10. two

BATTLE OF THE SEXES

1. False—a pizza.
2. Her mother arrived for a visit.
3. Four: They bowl, go to lodge meetings, play pool, play poker.
4. C
5. False—she goes to spend the night at the Kramdens'. (But before the night's over she's back upstairs—and Alice is with her!)
6. franks and beans
7. A
8. B
9. The "I-can't-stand-the-pain" sympathy routine, the "I'm-cutting-off-the-household-money" threat, and the "I'm-walking-out-forever" ultimatum.
10. False—he makes a beeline for the table full of food.

BETTER LIVING THROUGH TV

```
B E L L E V U E O P A Y D N A H
C H E F O F T H E F U T U R E O
H S C R E W D R I V E R M E A U
A C H E E S E G R A T E R M T S
R O S C L P H Z O N O T R O N E
L R C O R E A A P P L E S V B W
I K U R H A H A E T O L C E S I
E S T K O R S D N Y T E I C C F
C S G S J F U P C F N V S O H E
H K L C A I K O A G E I S R Z H
A A A R M S L S N L D S O N L E
N T S E A H H N S N M I R S J L
D E S W Z I P Z I P A O S X Q P
K K C H I N M O D E R N W A Y E
L E M O N G P J C H K S A M U R
B Y A T G S S C A L E F I S H O
```

THE SLEEPWALKER

```
T S R A P P L E P M N C E L Y B
K B M O P B A L E O B F S K Z A
M E N T A L C P N B D H Q J O N
K L N R Q O R E T T E S U B B A
O L T U V C C S A A G N I A A N
S S A Z O K O A T C I U R C D A
C H I C K E N C H O W M E I N P
I W T U N N E L O F L O V E N E
U P E E L S Y U L F U J D B J E
S W N T A W I N J H L W A R M L
Z A T A C K S T O S U I E J I H
K L H M C C L O S K E Y S N L S
O K A V S B A N A N A K F P K S
S I R Q R D N R O C P O P Q B T
O N Z S B J D I C K T R A C E Y
G G K U M Q U A T S L X Z T A C
```